King Crone and The Empty Nest

A Collection of TRANSformational Poetry for Rites of Passage

Keath Silva

King Crone and The Empty Nest

A Collection of TRANSformational Poetry for Rites of Passage

Keath Silva

ISBN (Print Edition): 979-8-35093-117-4

ISBN (eBook Edition): 979-8-35093-118-1

I dedicate this collection of poems to all the trans, non-binary and gender expansive people who are now living, those who came before and those who are yet to come.

Introduction

It takes some serious umph to nudge oneself through the heaps of day-to-day resistance and inertia, which has been hoarded to dull the pain of a broken heart. It takes a certain kind of desperation to bring oneself to the moment of actually sitting down to write the book. I am in one such moment, as I write this, which is hard earned and passionately savored.

Since coming out as trans, the challenging daily navigation of life as a neurodivergent and highly sensitive person has been much further complicated with problems which never touched me, while I was falsely wrapped, in the protective garment of presenting as a cis white woman.

The challenge of trudging through each day as a trans person, in a world in which people like me are largely erased and often actively unprotected, has made it difficult to carve out the time to focus on my craft. The labyrinth of obstacles that many trans people are slammed with on life's path, can be thick and heavy. For me, the urgent call of my poetry's need to be given, finally became stronger, than the tide I was pushing against to survive. So I am here. I am here to tell my story.

Every trans person has their own unique journey. Mine has not been one of feeling that I was born in the wrong body. I feel that I was born in the wrong world. As early as I can remember, I felt that I wasn't the girl that everyone was calling me but rather, something like a boy-girl or neither or both. I was mystified by being categorized into girl's clothes, activities, bathrooms and groups. I felt boyish and a delicious kinship with boyness. I also loved my body just the way it was and felt that it encompassed all genders and none, all at the same time. I believed that my body could be a happy place to live in, if there was a place for me in my community, if people could see and honor my inner experience of my gender. I only grew to hate my body because of the social response I was getting because of it.

Like so many of us, I was shaken out of the pleasure of loving who I was. I was robbed of the assuredness that I was okay. I always possessed the inner knowing that actually, everyone else was just confused in their confident belief that I was a girl, I knew who I was, but over time, even that was chipped away.

I chose to fit in. Rather than be harmed, teased, cast out, called horrible names and possibly much worse, I pushed myself down into the depths of forgetting and played the role of what the world believed I should be. Since I was trapped inside the confines of "girl" and "woman" and in urgent need of liberation, I did what I could within the parameters I found myself in and became an activist for women's liberation and power. I studied women's holistic health, herbalism, energy healing, bodywork and midwifery. I led circles of women, sang women's empowerment songs, engaged in moon rituals to reconnect ourselves to the healing power of nature and embrace our ancient wisdom. I went through my own years of therapy to recover from being socialized, molested, raped, drained, used, verbally abused, ridiculed and controlled as a girl and woman. I gave healing sessions to countless women who were also healing from abuse and oppression. I did this for many years, which was healing for me and for many.

All of these goings on ultimately lead me to remember and reclaim myself in my entirety which includes the fact that my gender expands outside of who I was told to be based on what was between my legs, on the day I was born. I eventually came out as non-binary and socially transitioned. After a few years, I legally changed my name and my gender marker to male and went through my medical transition, which for me only consists of hormone therapy. Now I identify as a non-binary trans-man. I feel jubilant about my gender identity and expression now, which is so settling for me and relieves the awful dysphoria I experienced for so long. I continue to offer my liberatory healing sessions to women (both cis and trans) as well as trans men, non-binary folk and people of all genders. I have traveled the whole circle and planted myself in a supportive community where I am seen and loved for who I am, as I am.

I am now a King Crone with a mountain of lived experience to share. I have had the hormonal ride of at least two lifetimes. This cosmic rollercoaster ride has given me uncanny insight into many aspects of human existence and I can now truly relate to so many different people's inner worlds and life's experiences. For this I am grateful. It certainly hasn't been easy, but I would do it all again.

I have had the joy of deep sistership, the awful pain of losing quite a bit of it, the blessings of menarche, motherhood, birth, postpartum, lactation, child rearing, menopause, the empty nest and fatherhood, the wonders of deep brotherhood, men's healing circles, the adventure of being a son and a daughter, then being delegated to "offspring" and the blessings of my non-binary buddies and trans community. My poetry is a celebration and a lifeline through all of that. May it touch you acutely in landscapes within, that you didn't even know existed, or had forgotten. I will let the poems tell you the rest.

Table of Contents

Ode to My Dead Voice

High pitched wonder
who never spoke up for yourself
rest in peace
like a Chickadee
finally free to escape
my chest

Top of the scale
pleading skeleton voice
who sucked back the scream
that suffocated your joy
rest in peace
like a whistle
nestled between
wet pursed lips

Meek and mild
accommodating one
who fawned and fixed
who betrayed your own heart

Rest in peace
like a crying child
who collapses
in benevolent arms
that gently hold you

Disembodied shadow voice
find your home now
in some desert wind
like a scorpion
caught under a glass
burrow into the sand
and fall apart there

There is nothing left
for you to hold up
or appease

Let this freckle face
tenor two lower boy
take over now
steering us all
to a voice that
wakes the hills
a voice that
pushes
swollen tender seeds
into the soil
and waters them copiously
with deep baratone love

Gender Euphoria

My life is so delicious
I just keep biting into it
and feeling the thrill
of exactly
what is meant for me
melting down
into
my
hungry
open
belly

Modern Access

My Ancient Trans Ancestors
think it is really cool
that I have access
to hormones
that support me
in expressing my inner truth

They call it "Essence of Boy"

They did it without hormones
yet succeeded
through
clothing and adornments
and living roles in community
which were in alignment
with their gender identity
and with much
community
respect
honor
and support

There was a place for them
in their human groups
in which they were beloved
revered even

They tell me that
people who didn't fit into the gender binary
were considered sacred
and were the visionaries
the healers
the ones the group looked towards for guidance
the message bringers
those who thought outside of the lines
and brought a fresh perspective
the deep nurturers and caregivers of young and old
the ones to bring fresh ideas
to their communities and families

They tell me that
Trans people are not a new phenomenon

We have always existed

Gender expansive people are not abnormal
Trans people are not divergent
Trans people do not have a condition that needs to be cured
Gender expansive people are not a problem that needs to be solved
Gender expansive people are an ordinary part of being human
People need to remember who we are
and reinstate the vital role we play in the human community

The fact that anyone has a problem with us
does not mean there's anything wrong with us
It means there is something very wrong
something very sick in society

Trans people bring the message of hope
that we can do better
that we can embrace the whole human family
that we can break out of the constraints of a violent society
that stamps upon a new born baby
who they are, who they can love, what roles they can have in society
what they can wear, what names they can use, how they can move,
how they can walk, how they can express, how they can feel
based on the anatomy between their legs

My Ancient Trans Ancestors
stand in a vast group behind me
in their glorious outfits
in their unbridled song
in their unfettered dance
with their medicine baskets
filled with healing magic
celebrating my every step
whispering their love for me
and keeping me strong

Boy Boobs

I love my binder
and I love my boobs
I love boobs in general
so this way
I have constant access to them
without bothering
anyone at all
I think they are cute
They are my boy boobs
but they get me into trouble
like kicked out of bathrooms
and getting called m'aam
or worse
so I contain them
these juicy round
pleasure filled bouncy friends

When I go out and about
my binder gets me
the sirs I need
fills my quota
then home again
we have all the fun

Testosterone Rage

I had always been a docile one
the fierce was strangled out of me
cuz setting boundaries wasn't okay
for girls
I was an appeaser
a sweet pleaser
providing reassurance
and nurture
to my abusers
to my keepers

I wrapped my rage
in cellophane
and tinfoil
and nicey-nice
and in - it's all my fault
and shoved it down
below my spine
choosing survival
and a roof
a meal

Then came T
when first he entered me
all became clear
I found my own self
residing in this body

What a homecoming it was
Oh!! Here I am! YES!

Some of the ones who stayed
told me they felt they were finally meeting me
for the first time
like I had been lost somewhere
(in a sea of estrogen)
until then

An edge began to grow
that protected me from feeling
responsible
for other people's
disappointment
bewilderment
anger
desire

No became a thing I had a handle on
and I could focus
I smelled like a goat
and took great pleasure in that

How hairy I became
and ridges grew on my skull
my voice no longer lost on the wind
descended
landed at my root

My clit woke up one day
and did not recognize herself
form and function transformed

Total bliss to be with my body
as it quit betraying me
and started housing me rightly

And then I lost it

It only happened once

I lost it
for the first and only time in my life
I released garbage piles of rotting stuck anger
It terrified me but felt so good

It was just something you said,
It set me off
I went in my room and locked the door
and an uncontrollable thunder shook my being
I started yelling and throwing things
I smashed and broke and destroyed
I could not stop myself
nor did I want to
I felt safe and knew I was not harming life
just stuff
I was giving life to all the parts of me
that were lost to convention

That rage that spent through me
like a locomotive
put years back on my life
I finally collapsed on the floor
with broken things all around me
and a big dent in the door

You peeked your head in
and needed reassurance
that I didn't want to destroy you
Nope
so you said you were a bit jealous
of the opportunity to let it rip

Pride

I pushed down my inner sense of who I was and lived deeply there
away from all of you
I used to wrestle with the boys

I was one of them
With my king snake wrapped around my neck gripping the handlebars of my dirt bike
tick-tocking on my skate board
until a familiar
friendly boy-punch at play made my chest
strangely hurt
and a little bump grew where his fist had landed

I said, "Hey! Look what you did to me!" But it kept on growing,
and then the other breast bud
joined in this unexpected betrayal

I tried to wash-off
those *trespassing* lumps
with 1,000 tears in the shower
But they swelled into something
the boys blushed over,
giggled and grabbed at,
and because of their pointed presence, I was treated in a whole new way

Not sensing any footing, no semblance of agency

as who I *knew* myself to be
slipped through my fingers like water
I took hold of a poisonous power
offered to me on the daily
"I see you took your pretty pills today."
"I am going to want your number in a few years."

I wielded that pretty girl power

even as I detested it

to prove that I was something you wanted
someone of any value
who might not be killed
for another day
who might have the chance of being kept

I wielded that pretty girl power
to twist you into knots
to have a false strength of influence on a sinking ship
to break your heart
like the pain
of those teasing words
that ripped me apart

Dressed in white gloves
and patent leather shoes
I scowled
My very life seemed threatened by the impossibility

of me getting to wear a tux and to be the one to say "May I have this dance?"

I didn't have words
for the chasm widening between my inner world and the mask of survival I donned

When the teacher said,
"Girls on one side, boys on the other," my inner voice asked,
"Where then, shall I go?"

When I was seen kissing Jennifer in front of my gray locker
a circle of jeerers
threw dagger words

which ripped
to shreds
the awakening glimmer of my true essence which I had just tasted on her lips

"You dirty Lesbian."
"You are disgusting."
"You have the grossest cooties." "You stay away from us!"

A part of me died that day as I blotted out
my own fledging spark and started getting high, very high, and often

I gave my body
that had already betrayed me away
to boys
and men
for their pleasure

for the fleeting hope
that I would pass for "normal" that I would not be utterly cast out of all
warmth of humanity
just for being who I am
and loving who I love

This thing of who we are
who we know ourselves to be on the inside
cannot actually be driven
out of us

Each time
I got close
to living the truth
of who I am
something came to strike me down triggering the memory
of the teenagers
throwing
blade slurs
at me
by the lockers
And I would push it
all back down
and hard

This thing of who we are
who we know ourselves to be on the inside
cannot actually be driven
out of us

And one day
the closet has no door
so you burn down
the whole house
and you don't give a fuck what people think
But truthfully you do and it hurts every day to be told that
who you are

is not ok

But you are out
and you live any way
and you find people like you reaching out their hands and their hearts

This skyscraper pile of shove after shove has taken me years to uncover

And every pain-in-the-ass obstacle to tackle
every hurdle
every insult

every threat
every fear
has all been worth it, to live myself
as I know myself to be
on the inside

T Day

T day used to come
every 14 days
I looked forward to it
with dread and anticipation
I had to conjure up
memories of
being misgendered
and bullied
to psyche myself up
to stab myself
Sometimes I asked you
to sit with me
for the stabbing
and you put a care bear
band-aid on my thigh
Now T day is everyday
and it's gentle
I don't cry at night anymore
for a stash
and I don't cringe
at the sound
of my own voice

Misgendered

I liken how I feel when you call me lady or ma'am to being a balloon that
has been suddenly popped, an unexpected slap in the face
a jolt, a fright

a startling concern that maybe
we are living in different universes and therefore I am utterly alone, invisible and lost to the day

I feel angry when I am misgendered my heart races
because I have been
branded

stamped
labeled
boxed
denied access
to truth and connection
completely misunderstood
not accounted for, un-protected, not remembered

Being misgendered
derails my day
like a train knocked off its track a child falling off a swing
or a bird being shot in mid-flight

I try to shield myself
from being misgendered by staying home
not going to parties declining social invitations lowering my voice

wearing certain clothing
avoiding certain people, circles, towns, establishments procrastinating on phone calls
walking with a strut
wearing a pronoun mask, hat, shirt, button
and, still, the onslaught continues

Each time it happens,
the quandary faces me
Shall I defend and assert myself
thus enduring the excuses, the hostility
the falling all over themselves with guilt,

the explanations, the defenses
the cascade of them hating themselves because I exist?

Or shall I just take the blow, shrink,
grab my groceries and go?

They Gave Me A Wide Berth

there is a void
a lack of anyone
pushing back into me
echo echo echo
I am falling
who will call my name
throw down a rope
who will leave
some dirty dishes
in my sink
so quiet
like kitten paws
so empty
like a broken shell

Those Who Stayed

I always had a pack of girls around me
laughing and joking and brushing our hair
we shaved our legs
with grapefruit flavored shaving cream
and made prank phone calls

I always had a following of women
who I led in full moon rituals
and massaged back to their own voices
I blessed them
with basil, marigold and rosemary
sang their lost maidens home to their bellies
and drummed for them
as their babies crowned

I was fiercely dedicated to protecting women and children
and I honored my own body
and my cycles of blood and birth and croning
yet when I was alone with me
I felt myself to be a gentle man
quietly supporting
there was an outer woman presenting
and an inner man guiding
and another feral woman hiding

As I allowed
the gentle guiding man
to emerge
the outer woman crumbled
and the wilder woman birthed him

She is a fierce one and older than the earth

He was so young
and still angry, horny and muddy
from being pushed down so long
he got himself into teenage troubles
run by libido and suppression
and a vulnerable aching need to be seen

She held him through it all

His beard grew in
he got his name
his voice cracked
and dropped
he learned
how to ride
the testosterone stallion
with help
from his queer and trans siblinghood
and settled into his manhood

She embraced him

So many cis sisters backed away
like I had become the persecutor
the opponent
the problem

Man- they gave me a wide berth
some shared their bewilderment
and disgust and shunned me

They had wanted me for the space
I provided for them to awaken
the deeper parts of themselves
but couldn't handle it
when I did that for myself

I grieved so hard to lose my sisters
and continued to choose myself

Then there are the ones who stayed
I am so grateful
thank you for riding
the waves of change
and seeing my soul
for listening and singing to me
and taking long walks
amongst cedar and oak
swapping stories and tears
your presence is as cozy as moss
and endures over the years
like fire in my hearth
and chamomile in my cup

And dear new sisters trans and cis
who come into my life
so strong and free
I thank you all
and celebrate
who we can
all
be
together

The In Betweens

I love it when things
are over
I am always
secretly
waiting
for the end

I am holding vigil
for that moment
of returning
when all becomes
quiet again

A dragonfly
perches on my finger

I stand on the shifting sand

the crack in the door
lets through
a sliver of light

I hug you goodbye
I watch you
walk away

I relish
in my own company

My teeth bite hungrily
into my new beginning

The space between things
is my muse

My love is the snapping of the fire
as it devours wood

Even better if
the wood was damp
and fire's warmth
made its famished way
through this
weighty
stuckness

Combustion, disintegration, breakdown, switch

The undoing thrills me

The uncontrollable moving parts fascinate me

Who will come closer pushed by an unseen hand?

Who will go away moved by an invisible breath?

What will be removed
to make room for the miracle?

I walked very slowly today
for the first time in a long time

I didn't want to stop
this slow dance
of the nothing
and everything
In between

Fetish

I am going to ask you to pull yourself off of me
like clouds, you are wispy, expansive, floating
into my reverie and under my nails

I peel you off like dried glue shining
on my palm
and there you are again
wafting in on the wind

I am going to ask you to pull yourself off of me

Call your own energy back to reside
somewhere
near or in
your own body

I am not the life of you
I am a baby tree
looking for root room
and a view of the sunlight

I am going to ask you to pull yourself off me
so I can breathe
I try to get a sense of my own inhalation
when you -the ocean- come crashing over me

I am building my own little place
yet you -the moonlight-
shine through the cracks in the straw

Retreat
Please do your part
to hold your own longing

Letter to my Conditioned Self

Please stop rattling me
with everything
that must be done
It is a lie
that I'll feel better
when it's complete

Life is never neat,
wrapped up and over
One thing spills
into another
in a continuous
and messy
cycle dance

So caress my spine
in place of shaking my core
and demanding results

Hold me with your love
in my disarray
instead of
whipping me
into shape

Visibility

Oh Angels!
Watch over me while I sleep
The world is so precarious and
tilted on a spindle of broken dreams

The maroon thread we are winding
reaches into a cave underground
where the old ones are spinning it
by a glowing fire

Bring me to the window
of this house of white stone

Walk me to the edge of this bluff

There is no use in hiding
when sunshine's fingers
beckon me
to leap

Being Trans is Beautiful

We walk between the worlds
We see from all sides
We have faced oppression
Or death
We break barriers
We build bridges
We open the possibility
of authenticity
For every one

Trans Angels

I have so many trans angels
the ones who lived a long life
the ones who died too soon
each one a bright star
in a very dark sky

When the day seems like
too much to greet
they whisper,
"We've got you."

When yet another person
condemns me
for just being
who I am
they reassure me, reminding,
"Your Light is too bright for them to bear."

When I find my joy
they cheer me on saying
"We love to see it."

When I stand up for us trans people
They say, "We are so proud of you!"

When I feel hurt
my trans angels
comfort my heart

When I hold space
for my trans friends
and their tears
my trans angels
stand at my back

To my dear trans family
please stay with us
Please don't leave too soon

Alas If you do need to go
or are taken
may this gigantic love
hold you forever

We will remember you
and listen

Thank You My Allies

When you call me by the name and pronouns I adore,

you give me
a gentle warm hug
a hand up
a healing balm
a bright smile in the dark
a heart opening wink
a bouquet of Sunflowers
a Yarrow blossom circle of protection
a tender Rose of sweetness
years on my life
a burst of energy
the ability to focus
a nourishing sense of safety and belonging a happy memory
a warm cup of Lemon Balm love

When you call me by the name and pronouns I adore,

you give me
wellness, welcome and home

Thank You

Death of The Make-Believe Girl

Take yourself down to the river
and sing to the bones
of who you once were

Pull back your umph
from the marrow
in the skeleton
that sunk to the bottom
and lays rocking on
pebbles and sand

Feed her flesh
to the hungry fishes
and from the depths
take back your spark and gleam
letting her bones erode into silt

Release the abrasions
the anguish the alluvium
that twists your mouth
and clenches your heart
leaving only tiny blessing stones
sparkling in the river bed

Take this avulsion
as a good sign
of life waking up to itself
like the first nettles of spring
so sharp and green poking
out from the forest floor

Appointment

Yes,
see you tomorrow
at 10 am
Also,
please remind the staff
that I am male
and my pronouns are he/him
It is very stressful for me
to be called she/her and m'aam
which often happens
in your office
Thank you

Risk All To be Who You Are

Scrambling up
out of the dark
grasping for fading blades of grass
illuminated by weakened rays of sun
as they split and break apart

Cold shaky hands
reaching up and out
while from below

Unknown
wrinkled
soft hands
so gently
pull down
on ankles

The hum
rises up
from
the old
ones
body
calling
come
come
into the center
of yourself

Eyes wide
and searching
Not this
anything
but this

descent

until the sun slips
behind the hills
and fingers are
too cold for clinging

We slide
into the
wild
embrace
of
the
glowing
darkness
Home

Weaning

Once I watched my cat

just start running away

with her oversized kittens

hanging on her teets

they eventually let go

and found some kibble

and their own locus of control

I relate so hard to that mama feline

who gave her all to bring life

to nurture and protect life

and now is done

my dangling kitties only include

one teenager

who seems to have already let go

and only needs a watchful eye and a loving presence

It's the projects and causes and rescue missions

the oversized hats, the excessive obligations, the over responsibilities

dragging me down

So I walk in the footsteps of the wise mother cat

walking fast in the direction of my dreams

On the path to my delight

New motto:

If it's not fun and does not feel like a total yes in my body, then it is a no, period.

Moving to Los Angeles

Savor these moments

This gorge
is no longer
your home

Your departure
is already
in full motion

Yet linger here
like a long goodbye
to a beloved friend

Touch each autumn leaf
crush them in your hand
sprinkle the golden dust
on this holy ground
amongst the Douglas Fir
the Alder and the Big leaf maple

Bless this place that held you
through so many cycles
so many moons
shining through branches
of Oak and Pine
so much change
in abundant laughter
heart crunching grief
Dogwood blossoms
and frolicking springtime loves
so many mistakes
and so much learning

May the seeds
you planted here
bear nutritious fruit

May all the hurts be healed
in the morning pink of
the Grass Widow's beauty

May all the grudges be forgotten
in the wind that sweeps up the big river

May all the harshness of
hard earned lessons
be softened with Moss Lichen
and dew on a Wild Rose petal

May the sweet memories
of friendship ripen in your heart
like the taste of bright green spruce tips
poking through the cold sparkling snow

As you pack up your things
to leave eager traveler
let go of anything not needed
for the journey ahead

Walk one more time
on this mountain trail
to taste these Salmon berries
and to sing to these waters

Dropping your excited tears
into this inevitable flow
that feeds the Tiger lillies
on its way
to the same ocean
you'll live by
in your new home

Living Places Are Like Lovers

Living places are like lovers

There is a mild sense of betrayal
of the old place
when you take a new one

There is always a bit of the one before
inside you
As you feel the excitement
and novelty of where you are now

I found a bit of moss and lichen
in my hair
and heard the roar
of umbrella falls

As I woke
to this sun drenched
Hummingbird Hibiscus morning

My Queer and Trans Friendships

My queer and trans friendships
are my wealth
they fill me with
warm yummy feelings
like lemon drops
and sweetmeats
banana bread and butter
the smell of evergreen branches
warm rain on my cheeks
a candle glowing in my heart
but much better than that
they lift me when I'm down
and bring me back down
when I'm floating too far
Laughing with my friends
makes life worth living
deeply shared experience
a gentle roller coaster ride
not alone at all
laughing at the chaos
of it all
showing up
again and again
Like "Hey friend
How are you?"
Queer and trans friends
are protective and
bad stuff rolls off
like water off a duck
and the pond is crossable
with them waiting on the other side

Are You Scared to Fall Asleep?

Last night
I was present to the darkness
who held me like a mother
I felt a yawning love there
more gaping
than the Columbia Gorge
deeper than the deepest roots
of the old white oak
I touched the passage
from waking to sleeping
I breathed through
the daily small death
I've been frantically
scrambling
to outrun

Now that I have been there
I can tell you
there is an opening
at the top of the dark
an innocent window
I've been shielding myself from
with screens and empty pleasures
of distraction
every night
for decades

A doorway opens in the dark
this round soft gate
invites me
into
the boundless radiance
of my own starlike heart
and to the sweet relief
of no thing
the bath of endlessness
& luminosity

I place my hand
on the creaky faucet
and turn it lefty loosey
and I die
so sweetly
into the flowing embrace
of my life giving
boatlike dreams

JUICY

and the
torturous sorting
through
mountains
of unresolved
traumatic happenings
dishes breaking
sudden endings
low grade chronic verbal abuse
over years
of 2 steps forward
1 step back
begins
to
bear
fruit
and it's
    Juicy

Soul Part Found

There you are little one
the one I have been looking for
I cannot live without you anymore
I am sorry I pushed you down
every time you dared to raise
your frightened eyes
to let me know you
I am sorry I tried
to throw you away
your hurting
is ok with me now
little bird
you flew so suddenly
into this world of broken glass
come now
we will pick up these shards
and weave something that the sunlight can dance upon
we will move real slow
as not to make our fingers bleed
I will sing to you
and hold your aching gaze
while we sweep away the pieces
too small to keep
and I will stay
and we can look at petals
and inch worms
and talk about every little thing
I know you
did not

want to be here
when noone could see
your magical flight
and iridescent feathers
and how it hurt
when they spoke of you
as if you did not exist
and just how lonely
that is
to have no-one to help you
when people
break down
your door
and just tromp around
your newly found heart
fold yourself
into my sun drenched lap
let me braid your
delicate golden hair
and wrap you sweetly in this
silky gossamer moonlight
while snowy owl
hoots us back together

Why?

Transphobic people
do not want me on their team
or in their town
or in the world
because I have done
the inner work
to find out who I am
and they have not

And I have the guts
to live my truth
and they do not

1.

True Abundance does not come
at the cost of others

2.

I leave behind
a complicated scarcity
and step into
a profound
and simple
Abundance

3.

I
no
longer
Sacrifice
my
well
being
for
other
people's
opinions
of
me

4.

Just
Say
No
To
Stuff
That
Sucks

5.

It
is
so
healing
to be touched
gently
where it hurts

6.

Please don't call me brave
Please effort to make a world
where I do not have to be brave to exist

7.

You may now feel what one hand feels
as it caresses the body of your love
It is any hand past or future
Shall I let it come?
Yes, I say, Yes!

8.

Oh Sea!
I long to be with you
But that would only make me wet
and leave you unchanged

9.

EMERGENCY!
I
am
having
feelings!

Resilience

Thank you people
Who walked away from me
so I could walk closer to myself
Who told me to leave you alone
so I could learn to love being alone
Who harmed me nearly beyond repair
so I could find my deepest resilience
Who ridiculed me
so I could know my own worth without you
Who triggered my trauma
and pushed my buttons
so I could see what was in need of healing
Who shunned me for my self care decisions
so I could make them anyway
Who falsely accused me
so I could know my own truth
Who I left
so I could find my own way
Who I said no to
so I could say yes
to this brilliant life
I now live

Dear Men Who Refuse to Feel

Dear men who refuse to feel
I gift you back your pain
Your shrapnel
saturating my soft body
flies back into yours
this is not mine to carry
I am not the ground
for you
to leak into
I am not the holder
of your undigested shock
I am not the place
where you can store
your unfelt rage
your putrid swollen
held back tears
Man
I am not
your fertile womb
I am not
your nurse seductress
I am not
your friend
Do your own #%*#!! work
hold your own pitiful heart
coward
look within
this grief will not kill you
as you are trying

to kill me with it
this shock will not end you
as you are trying to obliterate yourself
through exploding into me
Desperately seek
your inner boy
who shakes with terror
take your big warm hand
off my breast
and hold him
until he receives
your love

New and Old Me Meeting

In the soggy
waning light
I sang
my voice meeting
the cascading thunder
of the waterfall
and I saw them
my former self
sitting like they used to
behind the wall of water
and we met eyes

I'll be Right Here

When I was a child
the tiny petals drew me
into their luscious hue
into myself

My father
told me to hurry
and leave my flower
to keep up with his pace

and each time I left
I broke my own heart
to chase his unavailability
hoping somehow
to catch his eye
to someday
catch his heart
by quickening my step
by tearing myself away

But this time was different
I said to him
"You go on without me.
I am going to stay
Right here."

Parenting a Teen

After a while they don't need you anymore
Sometimes that means you did a good job
Sometimes it doesn't
They need to push against you
and away
to find their own footing
Even as the shore pulls at the sea
So step back
toss them a sandwich
(if they ask for one)
And pray

Coming Out

Oh Dark Night Sky
I put my feet
in your silky hands
There is nothing
left for me
in these impressions
I try to make
these lines
I strive
to stay within
All I want now
is for you
to backflip me
out of falsity
through the cold cutting air
to a place
where roots grow
from my feet
and warmth is there
for the holding

a Message for Trans Youth

There are many who come before you
We are shining bright
Holding you in our warmth
We are working
To make
The world a place
Where you can smile, live, play
And be celebrated
Until then
Tend the flame
Of who you are
In your wild creative hearts
Find us
And those who walk beside you
Together we will overcome
The world needs your light

Thriver

If your road had been easy
You would not have been
tempered cured and seasoned

Your heart would not be radiating
such juicy love through the cracks
and windows of this tender skin

Trans A Pause

I loved my bloodiness
the smear on my leg
the rusty smell
red drops on my sheets
the ache of longing
the weird mind space

That blood brought my babies to me
and took away ones that weren't meant to be

I waited until she was done
I gave her, her full ride

We had our bloody moon rites
all the dreams and visions she birthed
we had our hot water bottle
ginger tea
and candles
we had our hot flashes
erratic cycles
night sweats
we had our fear of being pregnant again
when she wouldnt come
and sweet yellow dock molasses syrup

I gave her, her full ride
but she came back
a few times
to assert her red power
after T came on board

We had a premenstrual T situation
like a tug of war
like a push and pull
like being dragged
in opposite directions
like losing my mind

She was going out with a bang
wrestling mood swing nausea nightmare
but we upped the T
and he won

Questions Some Trans People Ask Themselves

Shall I dress today to pass and be safe or to express my true self and be happy?

Which bathroom shall I use?

Do I really need to go that bad?

Is it worth the risk?

Which states shall I never go to again?

Is this symptom due to my hormone levels?

Is my testosterone too high and converting back to estrogen?

Will my insurance cover my care?

Will I be shot at an event celebrating my community?

Will I run out of hormones before I untie all this red tape for access?

Is it safe to walk alone?

Will I be misgendered?

How long do I have to wait before I can get surgery?

Am I passing?

Am I safe?

Will I be welcomed here?

Is it safe to go home for the holidays?

Will I need to educate my doctor?

Should I choose my truth or my safety in this situation?

Have I been wearing my binder too long?

Do they know I am trans?

Will I lose my job if they know I'm trans?

Should I go stealth to try and get hired?

Is this appointment or class to help me
going to end up being more traumatic
and exhausting
and draining
than the original problem?

Is it worth living in a world
where I am bullied
and laws are being made
to disappear me?

TSA

I used to really like to go on a trip

now it's pretty stressful

if it involves flying

I dread the TSA check

I scheme and plan the best way

to avoid being harrassed

If they set the scan on male

my chest sets off the alarms

If they set the scan on female

my groin sets off the alarms

Sometimes there is confusion

Sometimes there is ridicule

Sometimes there is groping

Always there is an ordeal

Kind of makes me want to stay home

The Stashes and Beards I've Made

Felt
Wool
Yarn
Mascara
Minoxidil
Eye liner
Eye shadow
Hair from my head
Craft hair
Faux fur
Inject T

End of My Rope

Thank you
for allowing me
to sit in the center
of your skull
just curled
like a little fiddle head
pulling inwards
until
I actually
can breathe
again

Thank you
for not stopping me
as I ever so slowly
approach
the windows of your eyes
and trace their sharp smooth edges
with my hungry palms
and twist my feet
feeling my way through
your nostrils
to let my legs
dangle and swing

Leaning my face
against the cool bone
I don't want to push anymore
I just want to be small and sweet
in the quiet of your loving me

Thank you for not telling me
to hush when I begin to hum
the sound of pain
that rises up
from my navel
and reverberates
in your mind

Oh the world is too much for me

Protect me

Remind
me
why
i
came
here
and why
It
makes
sense
for me
to
stay

The No Club

Welcome to the No club
Here is your knife
see the spiral and the word NO
carved on its handle?

The spiral is for the life death life cycle
allow what needs to die to die
which brings forward new life
This knife is a tool for you
to cut out what distracts you
from who you are
and what you came here to do
Your no is kind

Your boundary is beautiful
make room for
your soul's
flourishing

Hold the seeds of your destiny
in your cupped hand
It is time to make space
and nourish the ground
for the planting

Return To Center

When did I put you aside
oh tender one
with so many needs?

In winter you were
my guiding principle
and what a joy sprung from this

Summer pulled me out of my cave
and asked me to catapult
full throttle into doing
and your place at the center
seductively got taken over by
who I could be for others
as the days show up short
and there's a nip in my step
denying you is painful
so I call you to return
to your rightful place
in the middle of my heart

and when you whimper
"I am hungry"
I feed you

New Body New Community
A Better Fit and Still a Shock

I just want to go home
I need someone or something to attach to
It is like I've been floating or have been shook
while everything is changed in me
while all the lies are extracted from me

I am an empty seed pod
needing to fall to the ground

Let me melt back into dirt
let me rest

Let me hear a familiar voice
let me lean against the rough bark
of Ponderosa Pine
the same pine
with known lines and curves
to trace with my hand

I am tired of being anonymous
and spread so thin
please give me a moment
please give me a moment to grieve
all that has gone by
so fast

Pause here
collect me
lay me in your harvest basket
penetrate me with those golden eyes of love
I cannot do this alone anymore

Braid moss and yarrow into my hair
breathe your prayers into my brow

We are
so far from home
tuck me in
whisper my name
crack this rubbery shell

I am weary of bouncing
I long to just shine quietly
in this nest

Help me sort out all this excess furniture and photos and plates
I want to sit down and eat some clear soup

Touch my forehead
tell me
there there now
touch me
here here now

Perpetrator

The worst part of being trans in this society

is people fearing that I'll hurt their children

This one is hard to stomach

I am a gentle soul

I know first hand
the devastating harm abuse can do

There is a twisted wrongness

in your assumption

that trans people are somehow

perverse

Men's Circle

I was shattered
like glass
each shard
holding a precious part of me
every fragment
remembering the scene of the disaster

The blow that cracked me
each sliver having eyes
that see between
the fibers that weave
somebody together

The men that broke me
with their acrid sweat
their intoxicated want
their stumbling pursuit
their rotting entitlement
had a desperate need
to return to the tender petals
they denied in themselves
from very young boys
each time they moved with a flow
chose a color for their toes
felt the texture of silken scarves
older men pushed them down
naming them sissies
hardening
their tender sweetness
into brutality

There is a oneness
in being smashed
and scattered to the ends of the earth
each cut is exposed to winds from all directions
hears bird calls from all corners
smells the scent of buds that open
on faraway Islands
turns on its access
unsheltered by a definition of self
thus unlimited
by a body
we hear voices of angels
and ancestors and trees
calling our names

Not all men are perpetrators
I have met the gentle ones

As it was the deep voiced people
who wrecked me
It is the deep voiced friends
that soothe my being
with a connection grown from a mutual desire
to reclaim *the flowers that were ripped from us*

With a love sewn
from a shared experience
of unbearable pain
each time these men
the gentle ones
come to me
and show me their underbellies
another splinter of my devastated soul
finds it's position
becoming a brilliant facet
in the diamond
of my radiant heart
with roots

For A Sister Who Stayed

I like walking with you
because we pause along the path
and crouch beholding
tiny yellow violet faces
emerging from the forest floor

With delight
we slow our steps to ponder
the precise way spring water
drips off a mossy rock

We talk in circles and squares
connecting dots that previously seemed
unrelated and random
we converse in spirals and swirling zig zag patterns
weaving new pathways of mind
Sewing quilts the shape of the lives
we lived before we met one another
Here is where the tender used to be hidden
Soft spots are revealed
And caressed with balmy words
of reassurance and
"Of course you did!"

With each turn of the trail
another cliffhanger is revealed
yet I am calmed
trusting that we will hike again
and in time the unanswered questions
and the loose ends
will all be caught
and folded into these
knots of friendship
as the years pass

I like walking with you
because when we reach the top of the ridge
we each go to our own places
while you sit on a log in the sunny wide open
I nestle up against a cool
enveloping rock
where my mind careens
in the sight of
bare burnt trees
standing as white skeletons
on a pale blue sky
half-moon perched
in one of the hollow branches
I am lulled to the ground
between the fountaining bear grass
and glowing mariposa lilies
and I dream backward
to the time of cold and snow
on this longest day of the year
and forward
when the earth
will call
us to contract
once again

I am in both
deepest withdrawal
and brightest expansion
all at once

As the wheel of the year
turns forward and back
As the moon rests opaque
between new and full
On this summer solstice
on this steep mountainside
all of time is spinning at once
as the wind cries and laughs
like a thousand children
running to their freedom

It Is Not About me

Everything fell into place
and in an instant I knew
that you not looking me in the eye
that you not bringing me your warmth
had nothing to do with me
All along

I was just a bright little light
shining beyond
the cage
you keep yourself in

Brilliance

Do you know why there is so much adversity against you?

It is not because you are a bad person
It is because you are a bold person
It is because you grow and shine
and your heart is so huge and righteous

The world is dense
a bright light like you causes friction
so don't take their fearful bullying
their aggression
as a statement of your unworthiness
but rather as a testimony to
Your brilliance

Prayer

I pray
that the world
becomes a place
where it is safe
to be ourselves

Resources to support trans lives

Support Black Trans Lives: @Unique Woman's Coalition

Support Trans Latinas @The Trans Latin@ Coalition

Support Indigenous LGBTQIA people: https://www.niwrc.org/resources/toolkit/reconnecting-native-teachings-and-creating-healing-spaces-and-2slgbtq-victim

Support Asian American Trans People: https://pflag.org/events/asian-american-pacific-islander-community/

Support, Education and Advocacy for Trans people and their families: https://pflag.org

Trans Ally/ Trans parenting Workshops and coaching: https://www.transintimate.com

Free Gender Liberation Zine: https://www.keathsilva.org/fire-heart (scroll down)

My other book of trans poetry: https://www.keathsilva.org/ladydeath

Our Trans Loved Ones: https://pflag.org/wp-content/uploads/2023/01/OTLO_2019.pdf

The movie Disclosure: https://www.disclosurethemovie.com/about

For Practitioners working with trans people: https://www.amazon.com/Clinicians-Guide-Gender-Affirming-Care-Nonconforming/dp/1684030528

Non-Binary Empowerment: https://www.alokvmenon.com

Empowering Clothing/ Trans Artist: https:www.marswright.com

Trans advocacy in schools: https://www.theadvocateeducator.com

Trans Inclusive Children's Book: https://socialjusticebooks.org/i-am-jazz/

Trans Vocal freedom Courses: https://www.orionjohnstone.com/communitycoachingandworkshops/vocal-freedom-foundations-and-explorations-autumn-2021-hgzj8

Trans Chorus of LA: https://transchorusla.org

Keath's website: http://www.keathsilva.org

Keath's instagram: https://www.instagram.com/keathsilva/ and https://www.instagram.com/transmanpoet/

Support Trans Youth/ The Trevor Project: https://www.thetrevorproject.org

Training for creating trans inclusive spaces https://www.transeducation.net

Support Trans Youth @mermaidsgender on Instagram and 808-801-0400

Trans Health Care access info in California: https://askariana.com

About The Poet

Keath Silva is a non-binary trans man living in Los Angeles. He enjoys hiking, gardening, time with friends and family and writing poetry with his cats nearby. He has a private healing practice and sings in The Trans Chorus of Los Angeles.